MESMERIZED

HOW
BEN FRANKLIN
SOLVED *a* MYSTERY *that*
BAFFLED *All of*
FRANCE

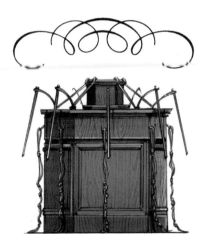

written by MARA ROCKLIFF

illustrated by IACOPO BRUNO

CANDLEWICK PRESS

1776

While the American Revolution raged at home, Benjamin Franklin sailed to France. His goal? To charm young King Louis the Sixteenth and Queen Marie Antoinette. Ben wanted them to send money and soldiers to America. The ragged, hungry revolutionaries needed France's help. Without it, they might lose the war. The king and queen of France were rich and powerful. But it turned out that they needed Ben's help, too. . . .

Philadelphia

For Jennifer Laughran,
agent *formidable. Merci beaucoup!*
M. R.

For Francesca,
my beloved *autre moitié*!
I. B.

First edition 2015

Library of Congress Catalog Card Number 2014939337
ISBN 978-0-7636-6351-3

14 15 16 17 18 19 TLF 10 9 8 7 6 5 4 3 2 1

Printed in Dongguan, Guangdong, China

This book was typeset in Bulmer, Bickham Script, and Officina.
The illustrations were drawn with pencil and colored digitally.

Candlewick Press
99 Dover Street
Somerville, Massachusetts 02144

visit us at www.candlewick.com

EUROPE

ATLANTIC OCEAN

Paris

MARIE ANTOINETTE AND KING LOUIS XVI

The day Ben Franklin first set foot in Paris, France, he found the city all abuzz. *Everyone* was talking about something *new* —

REMARKABLE
THRILLING

and
STRANGE.
Something called . . .
SCIENCE.

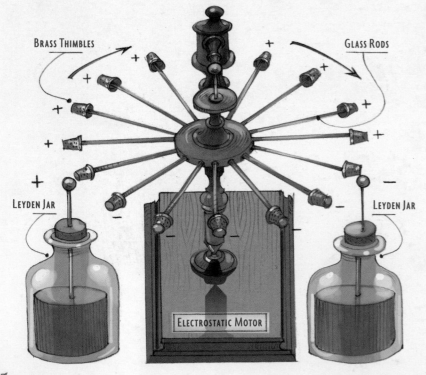

BRASS THIMBLES

GLASS RODS

LEYDEN JAR

LEYDEN JAR

ELECTROSTATIC MOTOR

Parisians giggled at a gas that nobody could see — till it went up in flames.

Voilà!

They gasped at the balloon that floated high above the rooftops carrying a duck, a rooster, and a very nervous sheep.

Oh la la!

And they went absolutely gaga over the American in the peculiar fur hat. Because *everyone* had heard about Ben Franklin's famous kite experiment, which showed that lightning was the same as electricity.

Mon cher papa!

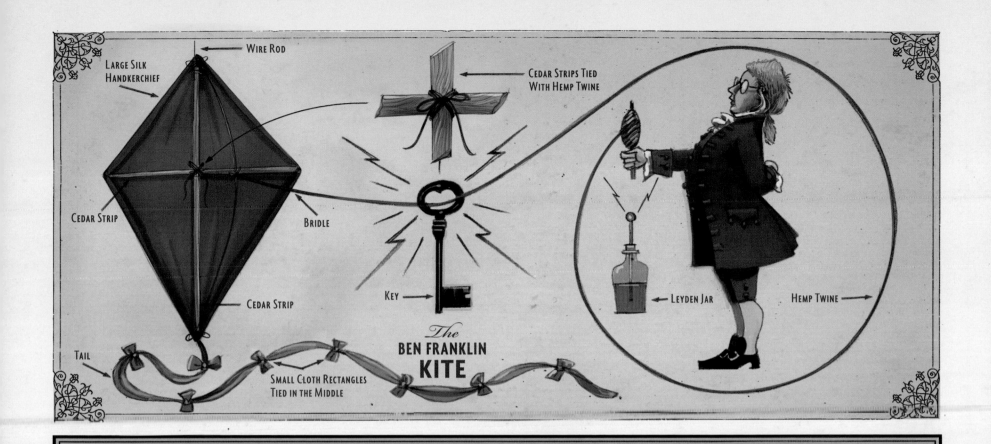

The Ben Franklin **KITE**

- Wire Rod
- Large Silk Handkerchief
- Cedar Strip
- Bridle
- Cedar Strip
- Cedar Strips Tied With Hemp Twine
- Key
- Leyden Jar
- Hemp Twine
- Tail
- Small Cloth Rectangles Tied in the Middle

THE SCIENTIFIC METHOD

BENJAMIN FRANKLIN

Ben **OBSERVED** lightning flashing across the sky. He **HYPOTHESIZED** — made a thoughtful guess — that it was electrical. Then he **TESTED** his guess by flying a kite during a thunderstorm. The kite had a metal wire at the top to attract lightning. The lightning ran down the kite's wet string into a metal key, where it made sparks — **SUPPORTING** Ben's hypothesis that it was electricity!

But soon all Paris was abuzz about somebody new.
Someone *remarkable*—*thrilling*—and definitely *strange*.
Someone called . . .

Dr. MESMES

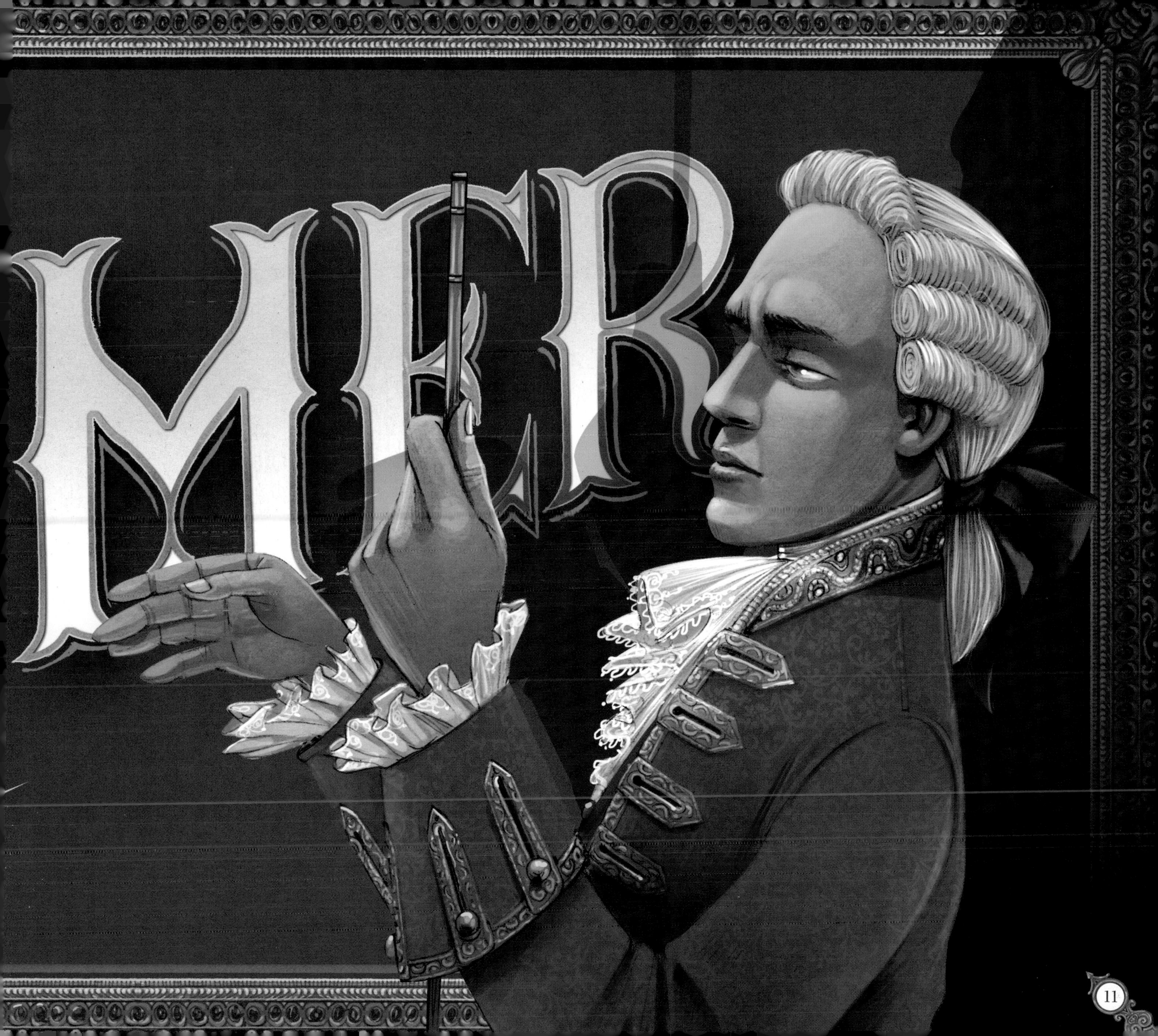
MER

Dr. Mesmer was as different from Ben Franklin as a fancy layered torte was from a homemade apple pie.

Where Ben was

PLAIN and SIMPLE,

APPLE PIE

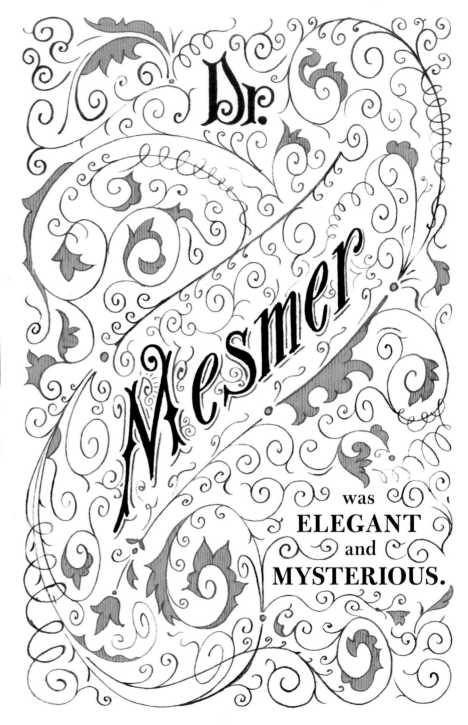

Dr.

Mesmer

was **ELEGANT** and **MYSTERIOUS.**

He wore a powdered wig and a fine coat of purple silk. He carried an iron wand. And he claimed to have discovered an astonishing new force.

Like a gas, this force could not be seen or touched. Like electricity, it held great power. Like the hot-air balloon, it made what seemed impossible come true. Dr. Mesmer said this force streamed from the stars and flowed into his wand. When he stared into his patients' eyes and waved the wand, things *happened*.

Gas

Electricity

Hot-Air Balloon

———⇥•◦•⇤ Women swooned. ⇥•◦•⇤———
Men sobbed.
Children fell down in fits.

Dr. Mesmer could make the same glass of water taste like twenty different things. If he told a patient to taste strawberries, the patient tasted strawberries.

Merci!

If he told the patient to taste vinegar, the patient tasted vinegar.

PHHHHHHT!

Dr. Mesmer said his force helped people who were sick. What kind of sickness? Any kind! Soon, everybody wanted to be *mesmerized*.

Dukes and countesses arrived in carriages at Dr. Mesmer's door. They disappeared into a room hidden behind heavy drapes covered with signs and symbols. Hours passed. At last, they came out and announced that they were . . .

C U R E D !

Bankers dropped their money bags. Lawyers flung down their books. Priests slipped away from their pulpits. Everybody crowded into Dr. Mesmer's darkened room. He agreed to share his secrets, for the sake of science (and 100 gold louis apiece).

EVERYONE agreed that Dr. Mesmer's force was the most *thrilling*, most *remarkable*, and *strangest* thing that science had discovered yet!

Well . . . not quite everyone.

Doctors were furious. Their patients didn't care about regular medicine anymore. All they wanted was a wave of Dr. Mesmer's wand.

The doctors griped—
    and groused—
        and fussed—
           and fumed.

Dr. Mesmer's force was *not* like electricity, a gas, or the hot air in a balloon, they told the king.

 *Non? Au contraire!*

The reason nobody could see or touch it was . . .

IT WASN'T THERE!

The king was in a quandary. Were the doctors simply peeved about losing their patients? Or was it true? Could all of Paris have been fooled — even the queen?

Je ne sais pas!

The king didn't know what to think. But he knew whom to ask. Who else but . . .

Ben Franklin!

SNAP!

Ben said he needed to see for himself what Dr. Mesmer's force could do.

IMPOSSIBLE!

I can do it, Dr. Mesmer!

Merci beaucoup, Charles!

Ben watched a group of patients being mesmerized by Dr. Mesmer's helper, Charles. They gasped and groaned — twitched and trembled — even fell down in a faint. Then it was Ben Franklin's turn. He didn't gasp and groan or twitch and tremble. And he didn't faint. In fact . . . he didn't feel a thing.

THE SCIENTIFIC METHOD

Ben **OBSERVED** the difference between the patients' reactions and his own.

DR. MESMER said that *l'américain* must be special. The force didn't work on him.

Ben had a different idea.

20

What if the force was not in Dr. Mesmer's wand — but in the patient's *mind*? Those patients *believed* the force was real. They *expected* to tremble and twitch — to gasp and groan — and to feel better. So they *did*!

THE SCIENTIFIC METHOD

Ben **HYPOTHESIZED** that what the patients felt was caused by their own minds, not by an invisible force.

But how could Ben be sure?
He watched another patient being
MESMERIZED.

Charles waved his fingers near
her face, and she screamed.
She said she felt a burning flame!

He never touched her.
But wherever his hand moved,
she felt the same fiery heat.

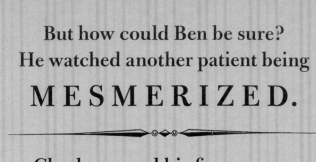

THE BAQUET

Ben asked her to try it once again . . .

Blindfolded.

When Charles waved
his fingers near
her STOMACH,
the patient cried
out in pain.
She said she felt
the heat—
IN HER EAR!

When Charles moved
behind her BACK,
the woman shrieked that
she felt burning—
IN HER LEG!

Ben blindfolded another patient.

Ben told him that he was being mesmerized.
The patient said he felt it.

Charles was not even in the room.

Then Charles came back into the room.
The patient didn't know he was there.

Charles stared at him.
He waved his fingers.
He pointed his wand.

This time, the patient didn't feel a thing!

THE SCIENTIFIC METHOD

Ben **TESTED** his hypothesis by blindfolding the patients.

Ben tested patient after patient, but it was always the same.

If the patient expected and believed something would happen, something did—
even *without* the force!

If the patient did not expect anything to happen, nothing did—
even *with* the force!

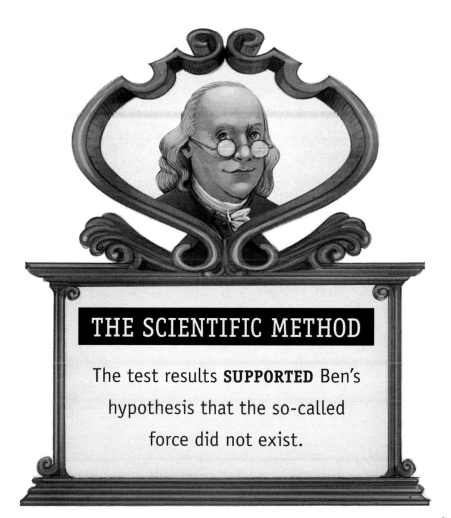

THE SCIENTIFIC METHOD

The test results **SUPPORTED** Ben's hypothesis that the so-called force did not exist.

Ben

went back to the king and

told him what

he'd seen.

Soon all of
PARIS
was abuzz again.

BZZ BZZ BZZ BZZ BZZ BZ
MESMER BZZ BZZ BZ
HA HA HA HA
HA HA HA
BZZ...MESMER BZ MESMER H
BZZ BZZ BZZ BZ
HA HA HA MESMER HA HA HA BZZ
BZZ BZZ BZZ
BZZ...

DR. MESMER
took his wand
and fled.

Not long after,

BEN

set sail.

Bon Voyage!

With help from France, the

REVOLUTION HAD BEEN WON!

F. PLURIBUS UNUM

Now he needed to get to work on
building a new nation —

The UNITED STATES

We the People

Article I.

Of course, he planned to find a little time for science, too.

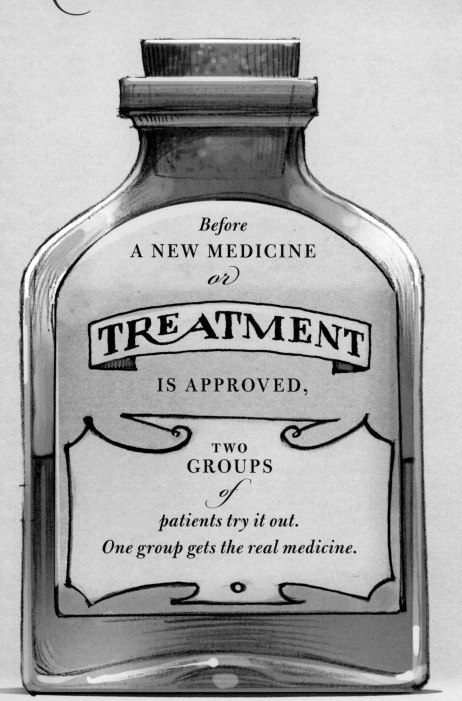

$\mathcal{B}$en's "blind" test was such a good idea that it is still in use.

Before
A NEW MEDICINE
or
TREATMENT
IS APPROVED,

TWO
GROUPS
of
patients try it out.
One group gets the real medicine.

The OTHER
gets a FAKE, *called a*

PLACEBO

The patients aren't blindfolded,
but they are blind in a sense,
because they don't know if the
medicine they took is real or fake.

That way, if the
group that takes the

**MReal
MEDICINE**

does better than the
placebo group, we can be sure
that the difference is due
to the medicine itself, not to
what the patients may have
expected or believed.

But what about people
who feel better after taking
a placebo? Think of
DR. MESMER'S
patients. . . .

Their
feelings were
real, even if the

FORCE

supposed to be at
work wasn't.

AND WHILE NOT
all of them

RECOVERED

from their illness,
MANY DID.

Although he never realized it, Dr. Mesmer had made an important discovery after all:
THE PLACEBO EFFECT.
Sometimes, a treatment works simply because people expect it to.

Belief can be powerful medicine!

And Dr. Mesmer helped his patients to believe. When he brought them into a dark, quiet room, stared into their eyes, and waved his wand, he put them in a highly focused state in which many people tend to believe and do whatever they are told.

Today, that state is called hypnosis. But we still use the word mesmerized when somebody seems to be in a trance. For instance, you might be so mesmerized by a cartoon that you don't hear your name when it is called!

Scientists are still learning about hypnosis, the placebo effect, and many other ways our minds can help us heal.

That would be no surprise to

Ben Franklin.

He knew that the mind could do amazing things—
such as using the scientific method
to find out the truth!

FIN

41

Oh La La . . . La Science!

BENJAMIN FRANKLIN first used the scientific method when he was just a boy. He grew up in Boston, by the ocean, and he loved to swim. Ben swam fast, but he observed that fish swam faster. He hypothesized that if he had fins like a fish, he could swim faster, too. So he tested his hypothesis by making a pair of thin wooden fins that fit over his hands. They worked!

BENJAMIN FRANKLIN *(1706–1790)*

THE SCIENTIFIC METHOD

1. Ask yourself a question about something you've observed.
2. Form a hypothesis (a smart guess) about the answer.
3. Test your hypothesis.
4. Observe the results and draw conclusions.

If the results support your hypothesis, you're done.
If they don't, revise your hypothesis and test again!

Ben went on to create many more inventions and conduct many more experiments. His report of flying a kite in a thunderstorm to draw down lightning made him the most famous American in the world. So when the rebellious colonies needed to ask the king of France for help against their common enemy, Great Britain, it was clear that Ben should be the one to go.

When he set sail for France in 1776, Ben was an old man. He suffered from gout and kidney stones. He had a double chin. Instead of a fashionable powdered wig, he wore a plain fur hat to cover his bald head. And yet the French treated Ben like a celebrity. Poets wrote verses in his honor. Fashionable ladies threw him parties and called him *mon cher papa* ("my dear papa"). So many souvenirs were sold showing old Ben in his fur hat and bifocal glasses—his own invention—that he wrote home, "my face is now almost as well known as that of the moon."

Ben Franklin's electricity wasn't the only mysterious force making a stir in France. Antoine Lavoisier, today known as the father of modern chemistry, dazzled audiences with demonstrations of invisible gases he named "hydrogen" and "oxygen." And in 1783, the Montgolfier brothers defied gravity with another force no one could see: hot air. Ben joined the eager crowd to see "Montgolfier gas" carry a giant balloon high over Paris. It landed in a field outside the city, where farmers took it for a flying monster and attacked it with pitchforks.

Meanwhile, in Vienna, a doctor named Franz Mesmer was also experimenting with invisible forces by waving magnets at his patients. Often, after this treatment, they felt better! Since doctors at that time favored treatments such as bleeding and purging, Mesmer's patients may have gotten better simply because he didn't make them worse.

FRANZ ANTON MESMER *(1734–1815)*

But even when he found he could help patients just as well without the magnets, Mesmer didn't question the healing power of magnetism. Instead, he announced that he'd discovered a new *type* of magnetism. He called this new force "animal magnetism" because it worked on living creatures just as ordinary magnets worked on metal.

In 1778, Mesmer arrived in Paris, where he began treating patients at a fancy hotel. The room was dimly lit, the windows hung with heavy drapes covered in mystical signs. The only sound was the sweet, haunting music of the glass armonica. (This instrument, which Mesmer loved, happened to have been invented by Ben Franklin!)

The patients sat in silence, holding hands around a wooden tub with iron rods called a *baquet*. The room grew hot and airless as the hours passed. Tall and elegant in his purple silk coat and powdered wig, Mesmer circled the room. He stared into his patients' eyes. He waved his hand across their faces until, one by one, they fell into a trance.

Mesmer's chief assistant and most enthusiastic supporter was Charles D'Eslon, personal physician to the king's brother. But other doctors did not share his enthusiasm. Annoyed at patients who demanded "the marvelous wand of *Monsieur* Mesmer" instead of regular medical treatment, they complained to the king.

When King Louis XVI asked him to take charge of investigating Dr. Mesmer, Ben

A GLASS ARMONICA

couldn't say no. The king had already sent aid to the struggling colonists, so Ben owed him a very big favor. And also, Ben was curious! He'd lived a long time and had seen a lot of "miracle cures" come and go. But Mesmer's ideas were spreading like wildfire. Across the ocean, General George Washington learned about animal magnetism from one of Mesmer's followers, a young French officer named the Marquis de Lafayette. Even Ben's own grandson wrote to him from England to say that he had joined Mesmer's secret society.

The king appointed a group of scientists and doctors to help Ben. This group included Antoine Lavoisier, the astronomer Jean-Sylvain Bailly, and Dr. Joseph-Ignace Guillotin, who was known for opposing the death penalty but also proposed replacing nooses, axes, and swords with a quick, painless machine. (Later, during the French Revolution, Guillotin narrowly escaped being beheaded by the machine that bore his name. Bailly and Lavoisier were not so lucky. Neither were King Louis and Queen Marie Antoinette.)

The scientists began with a question: Did Mesmer's invisible force actually exist? They soon discovered that their question couldn't be answered through observation. Animal magnetism did not shoot out sparks. It had no taste or smell. It could not be felt. And yet, *something* was causing Mesmer's patients to burst out with "piercing shrieks, tears, hiccups, and excessive laughter," as the scientists noted.

Ben's gout made it impossible for him to go to Mesmer's clinic — he couldn't bear the jolting of a carriage ride — and Mesmer refused to go to him. But Charles D'Eslon was happy to visit Ben's rented estate outside of Paris and demonstrate Mesmer's discovery to the scientists gathered there.

When Ben suggested blindfolding the patients, his fellow scientists agreed right away. (Lavoisier may even have come up with the idea first.) Finding that "imagination without magnetism produces convulsions" while "magnetism without imagination produces nothing," they reported to the king that animal magnetism did not exist. The "terrible, active power" at work on Mesmer's patients was their own imaginations.

Charles was dismayed by these results. Still, he argued loyally: "If the medicine of the imagination is the best, why shouldn't we practice it?" Mesmer, not so loyally, blamed Charles for doing it wrong.

Neither of these arguments did any good. Mesmer's secret society soon fell apart. Mesmer returned to his birthplace in Germany. There he lived with a pet canary that woke him up every morning by flying across the room and landing on his head.

Before leaving France himself, Ben managed to squeeze in a little more science. He wrote a scientific paper pointing out that a heavy fog across Europe the previous summer had been followed by violent hailstorms that winter. He hypothesized that the two might be connected, and suggested that his fellow scientists examine weather records from earlier years to put this hypothesis to the test.

As for Ben, he had another job to do — helping to write a constitution for the new United States of America.

SOURCES

Franklin, Benjamin, et al. "Report of the Commissioners Charged by the King with the Examination of Animal Magnetism" (reprinted from *Skeptic* magazine). *International Journal of Clinical and Experimental Hypnosis* 50, no. 4 (October 2002): 332–63.

BOOKS

Brands, H. W. *The First American: The Life and Times of Benjamin Franklin*. New York: Anchor Books, 2002.

Buranelli, Vincent. *The Wizard from Vienna: Franz Anton Mesmer*. New York: Coward, McCann & Geoghegan, 1975.

Gauld, Alan. *A History of Hypnotism*. Cambridge: Cambridge University Press, 1992.

Morgan, Edmund S. *Benjamin Franklin*. New Haven: Yale University Press, 2002.

Pattie, Frank. *Mesmer and Animal Magnetism: A Chapter in the History of Medicine*. Hamilton, New York: Edmonston, 1994.

Van Doren, Carl. *Benjamin Franklin*. New York: Viking, 1938.

ARTICLES

Kihlstrom, John F. "Mesmer, the Franklin Commission, and Hypnosis: A Counterfactual Essay." *International Journal of Clinical and Experimental Hypnosis* 50, no. 4 (October 2002): 407–19.

Lopez, Claude-Anne. "Franklin and Mesmer: An Encounter." *Yale Journal of Biology and Medicine* 66 (1993): 325–31.

Perry, Campbell, and Kevin M. McConkey. "The Franklin Commission Report in Light of Past and Present Understandings of Hypnosis." *International Journal of Clinical and Experimental Hypnosis* 50, no. 4 (October 2002): 387–96.

Schwartz, Stephan A. "The Blind Protocol and Its Place in Consciousness Research." *Explore* 1, no. 4 (July 2005): 284–9.

———. "Franklin's Forgotten Triumph: Scientific Testing." *American Heritage*, October 2004: 65–73.

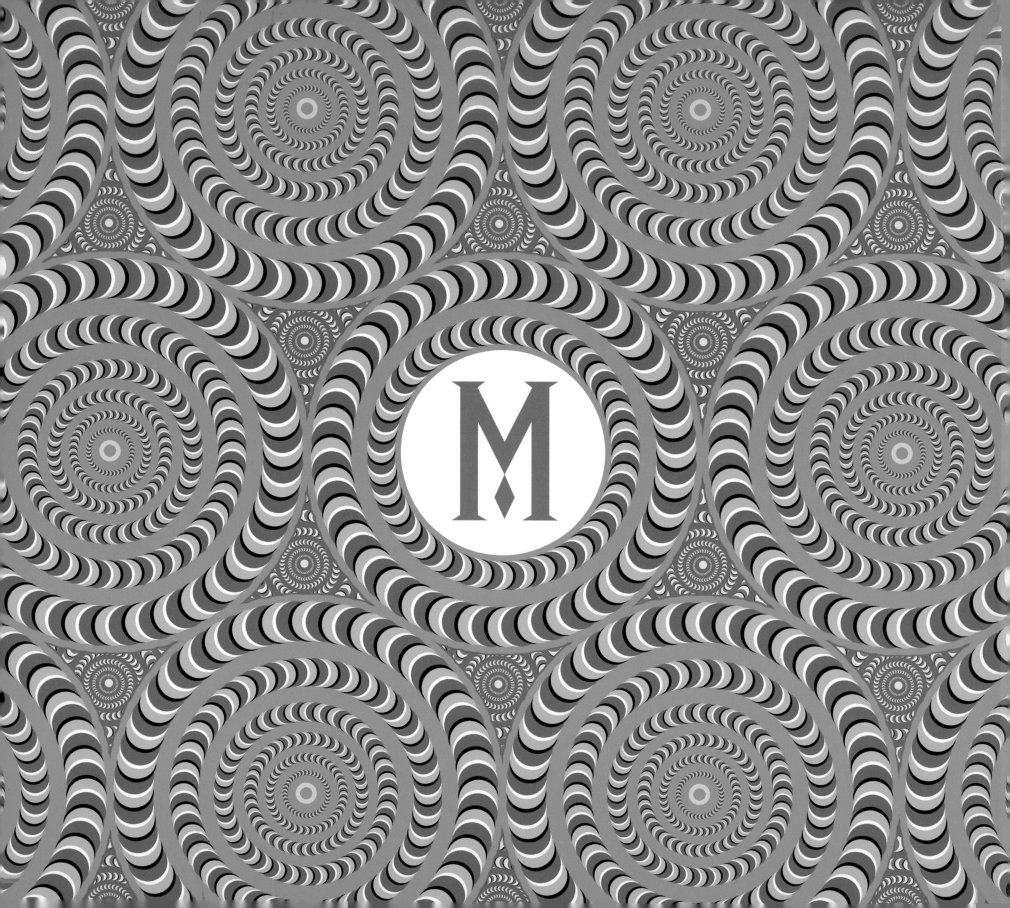